Life Cycle of a Guinea Pig

Angela Royston

Heinemann Interactive Library
Des Plaines, Illinois

Designed by Celia Floyd
Illustrations by Alan Fraser
Printed In Hong Kong by South China Printing Co. (1988) Ltd.

02 01 00 99 98
10 9 8 7 6 5 4 3 2

Library of Congress Cataloging-in-Publication Data

Royston, Angela.
    Life cycle of a guinea pig / by Angela Royston.
        p.   cm.
    Includes index.
    Summary: An introduction to the life cycle of a guinea pig from the time a tiny pup is born until, eight months later, it is fully grow and ready to start a family of its own.
      ISBN 1-57572-614-9 (lib. bdg.)
      1. Guinea pigs--Life cycles--Juvenile literature.   [1. Guinea pigs.]   I. Title.
    QL737.R634R69   1998
    599.35'92--dc21   97-39689
                                                                  CIP
                                                                  AC

Acknowledgements
The Publisher would like to thank the following for permission to reproduce photographs:
Bruce Coleman /Dr Eckart Potts p4; Lanceau/Cogis pp5, 25; Leibenswerte Neerschweinchen, Elrig Hansen c 1998 Kinder Buchverlag Luzern (Sauerlander AG) pp6–9, 11–13, 16, 17, 19–22; NHPA/Daniel Heuclin p24; NHPA/Jany Sauvanet p26; NHPA/Kevin Schafer p14; OSF/W Layer p18; South American Pictures/Tony Morrison p27 Testu/Cogis p15; Vidal/Cogis p23.

Cover photograph: Lanceau/Cogis

Contents

Meet the Guinea Pigs

A guinea pig is a small, furry animal with large front teeth. Guinea pigs belong to a group of animals called cavies.

Newborn

I day

I week

Capybara

The capybara is the largest kind of cavy. Wild guinea pigs are brown. The guinea pigs in this book are brown, white, and black.

1 month

8 months

10 months

Newborn

This female guinea pig is ready to give birth. First one tiny **pup** slides out. It is soon followed by another and then one more.

Newborn

I day

I week

The pups are wet and sticky, so the
mother licks them clean. The pups
open their eyes and look around.

1 month

8 months

10 months

This **pup** is still wet. She can see and hear, and soon is able to run around. She sniffs the hay and begins to explore.

Newborn

1 day

1 week

When she smells milk she pushes
her head under her mother and
finds a **teat**. Now she is having her
first drink of milk.

1 month

8 months

10 months

10

For safety, the **pups** keep close to their mother. This one is eating some grass with her long front teeth.

Newborn

1 day

1 week

A loud noise can scare the pups. They hide in the long grass until one of them pokes her head out to see if it's safe.

1 month

8 months

10 months

The **pups** play a lot. They sniff, rush around, and squeak loudly. They can even do a handstand!

Newborn

1 day

1 week

When they are tired they snuggle up together to sleep. They know their mother's smell and they know each other's.

I month

8 months

10 months

Wild guinea pigs are always on the lookout for danger. When this huge **condor** flies overhead, the little guinea pigs are terrified.

Newborn

I day

I week

Guinea pigs cannot run very fast
on their short legs. Instead, this
guinea pig stands completely still
so the condor does not see her.

1 month

8 months

10 months

Mating

The guinea pigs are fully grown now and ready to have a family of their own. A large brown male joins the group.

Newborn

I day

I week

He growls deeply and creeps around one of the female guinea pigs. The female sniffs his face and soon they **mate**.

1 month

8 months

10 months

New Pups 63 days later

18

For 63 days baby guinea pigs grow inside the female. She gets very hungry and eats more food. Guinea pigs like to eat juicy sweet corn.

Newborn

I day

I week

Then one day she hides away in the grass and her babies are born. She licks each one clean.

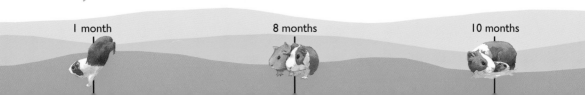

1 month

8 months

10 months

20

The new mother works hard looking after her **pups**. She licks them to keep them clean and soon they know her smell.

Newborn

I day

I week

She watches over the pups as they play in the straw. When she gives a special grunt, they rush to her to drink her milk.

1 month

8 months

10 months

22

The young **pups** keep close to their
mother. When she walks away,
they scurry after her.

Newborn

I day

I week

The pups grow quickly and are soon able to join all the other guinea pigs. Many new pups have been born and are growing up.

1 month

8 months

10 months

Wild guinea pigs have many predators. **Pumas** and other animals eat guinea pigs. Snakes, like this boa, also eat guinea pigs.

Newborn

I day

I week

This guinea pig is sniffing the air. She smells a snake coming and hides in the grass. Not all the guinea pigs are this lucky.

I month

8 months

10 months

Living with People

Wild guinea pigs come from South America. They live on the grassy **plains** and on the slopes of the Andes mountains.

These guinea pigs are kept by
people who live in the Andes
mountains. Guinea pigs kept as
pets may live for up to eight years.

Life Cycle

Newborn Pup

1

Pup

2

Pup

3

Mating

4

New Pups

5

Fact File

A guinea pig's front teeth never stop growing. Pet guinea pigs need to chew carrots or even a piece of wood to stop their teeth from growing too long.

A guinea pig is about twelve inches long – as long as a ruler – and weighs about one pound.

A female may have up to four **pups** at the same time, but she has only two **teats**, so the pups have to take turns feeding.

Glossary

condor   a large bird that lives in the Andes mountains of South America

mate   when a male and a female come together to produce babies

plains   flat, open countryside

puma   a large, wild cat that lives in the Andes mountains of South America

pup   a young guinea pig from the time it is born until it is old enough to look after itself

teat   a place from where a baby can drink milk from its mother

More Books to Read

Barrett, Norman S. *Guinea Pigs*. Danbury, CT: Watts, Franklin Inc.1990.

Burton, Jane. *Dazy the Guinea Pig*. Milwaukee, WI: Stevens, Gareth Inc. 1989.

Index